I love reading

Orang-utan Baby

by Monica Hughes

Editorial consultant: Mitch Cronick

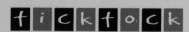

Copyright © **ticktock Entertainment Ltd 2006**
First published in Great Britain in 2006 by **ticktock Media Ltd.,**
Unit 2, Orchard Business Centre, North Farm Road, Tunbridge Wells, Kent TN2 3XF

We would like to thank: Shirley Bickler and Suzanne Baker

ISBN 1 86007 991 1 pbk
Printed in China

Picture credits
t=top, b=bottom, c=centre, l-left, r=right, OFC= outside front cover
All images courtesy of Digital Vision

CONTENTS

What is an orang-utan?

An orang-utan is a big ape.

They live in the rainforests of South East Asia.

They live high up in the trees.

Orang-utan

Asia

South East Asia

World map

Gibbons, gorillas and chimpanzees are also apes.

Other apes

Gorilla

Gibbon

Chimpanzee

5

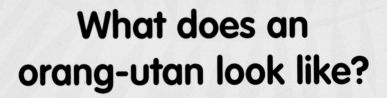

What does an orang-utan look like?

Orang-utans have shaggy, red hair and long arms.

They don't have tails.

A baby orang-utan has white rings of skin around its eyes.

A mother orang-utan

A father orang-utan is much bigger than a mother orang-utan.

He has big pads on his cheeks.

A father orang-utan

Meet a baby orang-utan

This is a baby orang-utan.

He is about two years old.

He lives with his mother high up in the trees.

The baby's father lives in another part of the rainforest.

9

What does the baby orang-utan eat?

At first the baby orang-utan has only his mother's milk.

Later he begins to eat fruit.

His mother chews the fruit.

She mashes it up in her mouth.

Then she gives it to him.

Orang-utan food

When the baby is bigger he gets his own food.

He eats figs and other fruit.

He eats bark, leaves, ants, snails and eggs, too.

Fruit

Ants

Snails

Orang-utans eat over 400 different kinds of food.

How does the baby get about?

The mother orang-utan has long hair.

The baby orang-utan holds on to her long hair.

He holds on as she swings from tree to tree.

When does the baby go off on his own?

When the baby is bigger he begins to get about on his own.

He holds on to a branch and swings to another one.

Then he swings from tree to tree.

Making a nest

The baby orang-utan sleeps with his mother at night.

She bends branches to make a nest high up in the trees.

She puts leaves in the nest to make it cosy.

Orang-utans in danger

Orang-utans live in the trees in the rainforest.

The trees are cut down for their wood.

When the rainforests get smaller there are not so many trees where the orang-utans can live.

If all the trees are cut down
where will the orang-utans live?

21

Thinking and talking about orang-utans

Where do orang-utans live?

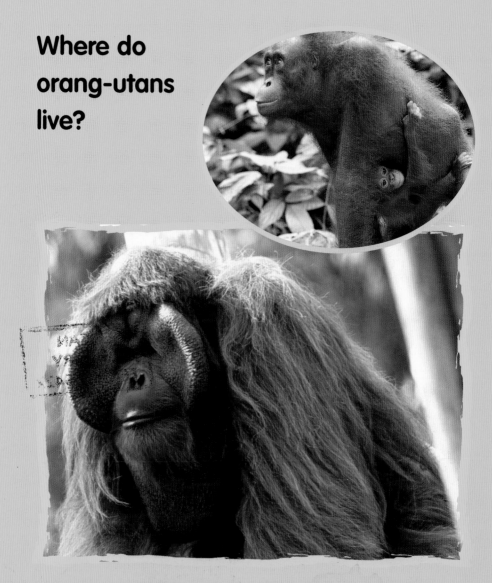

Who does the baby orang-utan live with?

How does the baby
orang-utan get
about?

Why does the
mother orang-utan
make a nest?

What would be the best thing
about being an orang-utan?

What might be the worst?

23

Activities

What did you think of this book?

 **Brilliant** **Good** **OK**

What was the most interesting fact you found in this book?

• • • • • • • • • • • • • • •

Make a big poster to show that orang-utans are in danger.

• • • • • • • • • • • • • • •

Who is the author of this book? Have you read *Tiger Cub* by the same author?

• • • • • • • • • • • • • • •

Look at the picture of the orang-utan's hand. How is it like your hand?
How is it different?